WEEKLY READER BOOKS presents

What Is Gravity?

A **Just Ask** Book

Hi, my name is
Christopher!

by Chris Arvetis
and Carole Palmer

illustrated by
Vernon McKissack

FIELD PUBLICATIONS
MIDDLETOWN, CT.

Hey, that hurt!
I wonder—
why do things fall?

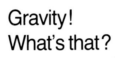

It's a very hard thing to explain. But I'll try. Let's start with the apple.

This is interesting!

When I drop the apple,
it falls to the ground.
Watch it fall.

Look out,
Christopher!

When I jump off this rock,
I fall to the ground.
You try it, too.

Gravity is the force that
makes this happen.
We cannot see it, and
we cannot feel it.
Gravity pulls things
toward the ground.
It keeps our feet
on the ground.

Just imagine if we lived in a place where there was no gravity.

Look at these pictures.

They show what it would be like.

See our friends floating in the air.

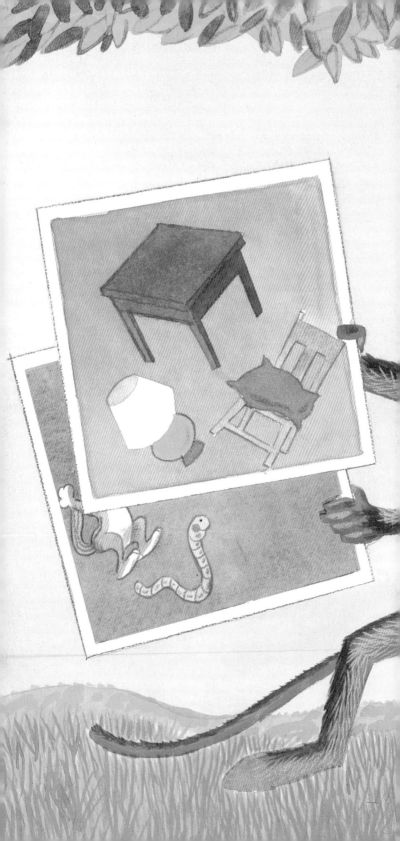

Everything would float in the air.
Look at the chair and table.
They float just like the animals.

Gravity on the earth keeps
us on the ground.
A scientist—
Isaac Newton—
studied about gravity.
He told us many things
about gravity.

Gravity also explains the way things move. Remember the apple? When I drop it, it falls in a straight line until it hits the ground.
Careful!

If I drop it and it hits this branch, it changes direction. Then it falls in a straight line until it hits the ground.
Not again!

Now, if we look at the apple on the ground, it will never start to move by itself.

Gravity holds it in place.

It will never move unless someone or something makes it.

We can see this if we look at a ball game.
The ball keeps on moving as long as the players are hitting it back and forth.

Once the ball stops, someone or something has to make it move.

Or gravity will hold the ball right where it is.

Gravity holds you on the ground and keeps things in place around you.
It is a part of our world on earth.